Written by Diane Costa de Beauregard
Illustrated by Cyril Lepagnol

Specialist adviser:
Dr Jane Mainwaring,
The British Museum
(Natural History)

ISBN 1 85103 051 4
First published 1989 in the United Kingdom by
Moonlight Publishing Ltd,
131 Kensington Church Street, London W8
© 1987 by Editions Gallimard
Translated by Sarah Matthews
English text © 1989 by Moonlight Publishing Ltd

Typeset in Great Britain by Saxon Ltd., Derby
Printed in Italy by La Editoriale Libraria

POCKET • WORLDS

Our Blue Planet

Astronauts, looking at Earth
from space, see a blue planet ...

The Earth looks blue because two thirds of it are covered with water.

Water makes up our hundreds of seas, and our five oceans.

Oceans are vast stretches of salt water. The biggest and deepest of all is the so-called 'peaceful' or Pacific Ocean, named by the Portuguese explorer Magellan. In 1520, he had just come through weeks of terrible storms which had almost wrecked his sailing-ship. Suddenly he found himself at the edge of a vast expanse of smooth, sunny water. 'El Pacifico!' he cried – 'the peaceful one' – the **Pacific Ocean** had been given its name.

Atlantic

Pacific

The **Indian Ocean** runs along the coast of India, the **Arctic Ocean** surrounds the North Pole, and the **Antarctic Ocean** surrounds the South Pole. The **Atlantic Ocean** lies between Europe and America.

Although the Pacific was calm when Magellan first set eyes on it, it can also be the roughest and most dangerous of all the oceans.

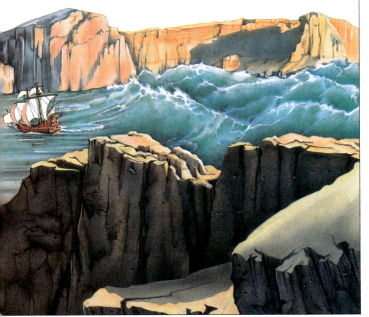

Round the edge of a volcanic island, minute sea-animals called corals live in bony colonies, each generation growing on top of the last, forming a kind of wall. After a while, more volcanic action causes the island to sink.

Another world under the sea

For a long while, people believed that the sea-bottom was flat and smooth. Then they discovered that it had mountains higher than any on land, with valleys and plains and erupting volcanoes.

1

Echo-sounders measure the depth of the oceans (1). Scientists transmit sound down towards the sea-bottom, and then measure how long it takes for the sound to be bounced back: the longer it is, the deeper the water.

Gradually, the island disappears beneath the surface of the sea. The coral reef remains, surrounding a lagoon of calm, shallow water: a coral atoll.

Some volcanoes burst right up through the surface of the sea to make new islands. They rarely remain for long, however; another eruption or earthquake makes them disappear again.

People have always dreamt of exploring under the sea!

But you can't go down more than a few metres without equipment: you can't breathe underwater, and the weight of the water presses down on you as you go deeper and squeezes your lungs.

In the fifteenth century, Leonardo da Vinci, an Italian painter and scientist who loved problem-solving, designed flippers and a mask with a breathing-tube. It took hundreds of years, though, before inventions like his were actually made and used.

Leonardo da Vinci's breathing-tube and flippers

The first diving-helmet, 1837

The 'turtle', 1776

⬥ In the nineteenth century, a French writer, Jules Verne, wrote a story about a man who lived '20,000 leagues under the sea'.

Nowadays, divers carry bottles of compressed air to breathe, so that they can spend long periods underwater.

Mini-submarines make it possible to dive down to even greater depths. They are used a lot for exploring, and for work like looking after the foundations of oil-rigs at sea. Some can dive down to depths of six thousand metres – not even seaweed grows as deep as that!

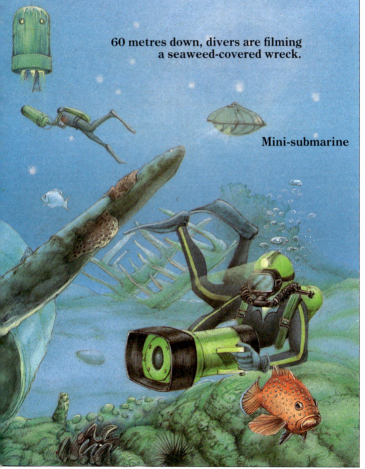

60 metres down, divers are filming a seaweed-covered wreck.

Mini-submarine

All the animals that live under the sea have their own place in the chain of life.

The first link in the food chain, plankton, is made up of tiny plants, called phytoplankton (1), and the minute animals which feed on them, called zooplankton (2). Fish like herring (3) eat the plankton. They in turn are eaten by tunny fish (4), who themselves are eaten by sharks (5). Small fish are eaten by bigger fish, and bigger fish are eaten by even bigger fish... Crabs and lobsters eat the scraps, while any shreds that are left over drop down between their claws to the sea-floor, to be eaten by the smaller animals that crawl about there.

Fish that live at great depths have very thin bodies and wide, gaping mouths.

There are many different plants and animals living in the sea. Each of them is specially adapted to its particular living space. **Coral reefs are home to many plants and brilliantly-coloured animals**. The corals themselves, the tiny animals which build the reefs, range in colour from pale orange to blue. There are 2,500 kinds of coral.

Green seaweeds live close to the surface. Lower down, algae are brown. At the deepest point, seaweeds are red.

Sea-anemones (1) live on the coral reefs. They are animals which cling to the rocks and look like flowers, with their bright colours and waving, petal-like tentacles. But the sea-anemones' tentacles sting. Clown-fish (2) live in between the tentacles. The stings don't hurt them and they tidy up the scraps from the anemones' meals. Sponges (3) live on the reef as well, in all sorts of colours and shapes.

Whales and dolphins (1 and 2) are mammals which live in the sea. They have lungs and need to swim up to the surface to breathe. Their young are born and suckled at sea.

Walrus (3), like sea-lions, are mammals too. They are covered with fur. They spend part of their lives on land, and that is where their young are born.

Seabirds like **seagulls** (4) hover over the surface of the water on the look-out for the fish they feed on.

Gannets dive for fish from great heights — up to 30 metres, the height of a lighthouse. They have very thick skulls, with air-pockets, which protect their heads from the impact.

The Gulf Stream flows in a clockwise direction. Ships follow it when they want to get to Europe from America, and avoid it when they want to reach America.

Currents and tides constantly swirl through the seas and oceans.

Every day, the sea rises and falls, drawn by gravity from the sun and moon – this forms the tides.

Currents are like rivers which run through the sea, always flowing in the same direction. They are created by the winds blowing on the surface of the water, by the turning of the earth, and by warm water meeting cooler water.

The warmest current is the Gulf Stream.

Fishermen discovered it a long time ago, following schools of whales: the whales swim alongside the warm water, but never go into it.

In 1947, a Norwegian sailor called Thor Heyerdahl built the Kon-Tiki, a full-size model of an ancient Mayan raft and floated it, following the Humboldt Current from Peru to Polynesia.

Seabirds resting on the surface of the water bob up and down on the waves. The waves rise and fall but do not move forward.

When the wind blows, it makes waves on the surface of the sea.
The waves go up and down. It looks as if the water is moving forward. But the water does not move forward: it is the energy from the wind which has been absorbed by the water which is going forward, pushing the water up and down as it passes through. A big storm can raise waves taller than a house. They come crashing down, foaming with spray.

Waves are born a long way from where they finally come ashore.
Waves raised by winds off the coast of America come lapping at the shores of Europe, 5000 kilometres away.

Only the surface of the water is disturbed by the waves.
Down below, the fish swim quietly in calm waters. Sometimes, though, undersea earthquakes create waves deep down which ships on the surface know nothing about.

Tidal waves are huge, dangerous mountains of water.

Some of them have been created by violent storms which whip up enormous amounts of water.

1   **2**   **3**   **4**

These globes picture the Earth at periods of time 50 million years apart. Scientists think that America is drifting away from Europe at the rate of 2 cm a year.

Tidal waves destroy everything in their path. The surface of the Earth is divided into seven main parts. These parts, or plates, are rubbing along each other at the edges, changing position slightly. When this happens, there are earthquakes and volcanoes. Volcanoes and earthquakes under the sea push aside huge volumes of water, creating a tidal wave which can rush over whole islands, crushing trees and houses on their way. The Atlantic Ocean is supposed to be named after the legendary island of Atlantis, which is said to have disappeared under the ocean after a volcanic eruption.

The South Pole is entirely surrounded by the Antarctic Ocean. It's the only place where you will find king penguins.

Polar bears live at the North Pole, where there is nothing but an enormous glacier.

Most of an iceberg is under water.
It may take up to 4 years to
dissolve in the sea.

Most of the water that
covers the Earth is salty.
**Most of the fresh water
that there is on Earth
is frozen at the
North and South Poles**.
These glaciers of fresh water, called sheet
ice, are gradually grinding their way
towards the sea. At the very edge, blocks
of ice drop off into the sea and form
icebergs (literally, mountains of ice).
Icebergs are very dangerous to shipping,
but nowadays ships can use a radar to
keep a careful watch for them when
sailing in icy waters.

Icebergs from the South Pole are flat
and float along like enormous
table-tops.

Icebergs from the North Pole usually look more
like mountains. They are tall, pointed and irregular.

We must protect our seas!

If an oil-tanker is shipwrecked and spills its load into the sea, the oil smothers and kills the creatures that live in the sea and on the coast. Some ships even empty their tanks deliberately to clean them while they're at sea.

This cormorant has suffocated in crude oil from a tanker.

People sometimes treat the sea as a rubbish-bin, tossing refuse into it from boats and at the seaside. But when we poison the sea, we poison everything that lives in it.

On board some trawlers, fish is still salted to preserve it as soon as it is caught.

The sea is rich in fish.

Fish is an important part of the food that we eat. In some countries, it is the main food.

As soon as it has been landed on board, the fish is processed ready for selling and eating. First it is cleaned (1), then washed (2), then frozen (3).

A trawler is a floating fishing factory. The trawl-net, which it drags along behind it, draws in huge numbers of fish from depths of up to 300 m.

Oil under the sea

There are huge reserves of oil in the rocks under the sea-bottom. As yet, people have only drilled for a small part of this oil. To reach it, towering oil-rigs have to be constructed, their strong legs resting on the sea-bed to hold them in place whatever the weather.

Diving for the riches of the sea

For thousands of years, men have dived for sponges, coral and pearls. Divers without air-tanks can go down to six metres and stay underwater for two or three minutes before coming up for air.

There are nodules rich in minerals scattered all over the sea-beds of the Atlantic and the Pacific, waiting to be used.

Metals under the sea

Every metal in the world can be found dissolved in sea-water – even gold. But they are difficult and expensive to extract. At the moment, only magnesium, which is used in building aircraft, and bromine, used in the photographic industry, are being separated and used.

The sponge is a marine animal. Its soft skeleton is the sponge people use in the bath.

A few rare oysters make the pearls which are used in expensive jewellery.

Japanese divers

The sea can be every blue imaginable, it can be almost green, or the palest greenish-yellow over the sand-banks.

The light falling on the sea and the depth of the water over different kinds of seabed make it all these different colours.

Greenish regions, rich in plankton, are full of fish.

When the sea is rough, it is white with foam made from air-bubbles trapped in the thrashing water.

When the sky is grey and overcast, the sea is grey; when the sun sinks, the sea may turn almost red with the sun's light.

Far out to sea, the deepest blue stretches are called blue deserts because there are hardly any fish there.

Index